WHEN SCARS BECOME BEAUTY MARKS

RACQUEL RICKETTS-LEE

Scriptures marked NKJV are taken from the NEW KING JAMES VERSION (NKJV): Scripture taken from the NEW KING JAMES VERSION®. Copyright © 1982 by Thomas Nelson, Inc. Used by permission. All rights reserved.

WHEN SCARS BECOME BEAUTY MARKS

Copyright © 2020 by Racquel Ricketts-Lee

ISBN 987-1-7332994-8-0 (pbk)

All rights reserved. No part of this publication may be reproduced, distributed, or transmitted in any form or by any means, including photocopying, recording, or other electronic or mechanical methods, without the prior written permission of the publisher, except in the case of brief quotations embodied in critical reviews and certain other noncommercial uses permitted by copyright law.

SOAR PUBLISHING HOUSE
New York, New York, 11212-9002
www.soarpublishinghouse.com

Cover Design by Keifer Simpson

Crossword puzzle generated at Education.com

Printed in the United States of America.

To my sister Lisa Orr,
the one who cares for me like a mother, advises me like a counsellor and always has a listening ear like a friend. You smile in the midst of adversity. You are the strongest woman I know. I love you.

Contents

Acknowledgements ix
Preface xiii
When Scars Become Beauty Marks xvii

The Scars Within

    Listen 1
    One Last Dance 5
    Sinful Nature 9
    A Seed Is a Seed 13

Mending in the Making

    She Doesn't Love Me 19
    Optical Illusion 25
    Dream 29
    The One Is Me 33
    Don't Lose Hope 37
    Faithful God 41
    Rest 45
    Prison Break 47
    Good Morning 51
    The Author 55

Beauty Marks

    What Mask? 61
    Judge Not 65

That Girl 69
The Lost Sheep 73
I am Beauty 77
Self-Love 81
Broken to Beauty Marks... 85

About The Author 91

Acknowledgements

Gratitude is a must, and for that I want to thank God for trusting me enough to deposit such a gift in me. I thank Him for anointing my hands and heart to write in a manner that will bring healing and restoration to the broken females within the Body of Christ and the wider society.

I would also like to thank the blessed Holy Spirit who comforted me when I became anxious about which poems to select for this publication.

To the Lees family, my husband Christopher, sons Dominic, Dimetri and K'Leb, thank you all for pushing me to be a better person, a great mom and leader.

To my support team, my mom Hazel Smikle, second mom Sonia Samuels, Clive and Pauline, thank you all for believing in me.

Thanks to my late father Seymour Ricketts who taught me to be tough and never to be surprised by anything. I pray that your soul found a resting place.

Thanks to my stepdad Alexander Smikle. You contributed tremendously to my childhood; you have shown me and taught me how I should be respected and treated as a lady.

I also express sincere thanks to:

Alia Wedderburn, my friend for many years, one who I can call upon for creative ideas and honesty, one who has been present from the conception of the idea and rode with me throughout.

My dear friend and church brother, Alfred Tulloch, I am grateful for your insight and the ways in which you challenged me to develop my gift.

My dear friend Stephanie Dunstan, we have been friends for most of our lives. Thank you for your unwavering support. Blood couldn't make us closer.

My prayer mother, Minister Winsome Briscoe-Casserley. Thank you for toiling in prayer for me and challenging me to be the best me.

Dr. Kadian Walters who prophesied to me 8 years ago and broke my mental chains.

My prayer partners, Chrisando and Shanna Kaye Christie, thank you both.

Mr. Keifer Simpson, for bringing my cover artwork to life. Thank you for your patience, creative guidance and influence. My publisher, Soar Publishing House, your patience and support were a great encouragement and motivation. Thank you.

Special thanks also to:

One of my spiritual fathers and mentor, Rev. Marcus Williams. Thank you for teaching me how to pray, praying for me and believing in me.

My spiritual parents, my pastor Reverend Norman Lewin and his lovely wife Minister Elaine Lewin from the Kingdom Builders Open Bible Church. Thank you for having me under your covering and pouring into me as a contribution to my spiritual growth and maturity. You are leaders who walk the way as true disciples of God.

Finally, thanks to you my readers for allowing me to enter into your intimate spaces through this book. May God use this as a medium to encourage, deliver and restore. As you read these poems, I pray that they will act like spiritual vaccination, eradicating all ungodly mental and emotional viruses. Let the work of restoration begin.

Preface

On the body, a *SCAR* is an area of fibrous tissue that replaces normal skin after an injury. A scar results from the biological process of a *WOUND* repaired in the skin. Scarring is a natural part of the healing process. It is easy to identify physical scars because of their visibilities. Sometimes the scarring can be so unsightly one would make every effort to cover it up.

I'm a certified Beauty Therapist and I've worked as an Aesthetician, studying the kinds and impact of trauma to the skin, as well as treating various skin types. Throughout the course of my work, I've made a number of observations—for example, I've noticed that new scar tissues usually have a different texture. The scar can minimize naturally or through medical treatment. In time, some collagen breaks down at the area of the wound and the blood supply reduces. The scar gradually becomes smoother, softer and less visible.

Physical scars can easily be covered up or removed through medical procedures and cosmetic products, but how does one treat an emotional scar? Like the physical scar, there is a replacement—normal healthy emotions turn into fear, hurt, rejection and low self-esteem due to disheartening experiences (let's call these emotional injuries).

There are a great number of broken girls and women in our society today. Some bearing scars from their early childhood. Brokenness causes you to feel insecure, steals your joy and causes secondary problems in any type of relationship. I am aware of the effects of brokenness and the impact it can have on lives because I have experienced it myself. I know what it does to a person. Those who have suffered any form of abuse or rejection, as I have, often seek the approval of others, become withdrawn or rebellious.

Having had these experiences, from the age of about six, my pencil and paper became my best friends. I can remember expressing myself, pouring out my heart on any piece of paper I got hold of. Sometimes the writings would be integrated with tears. There are many times while writing that I would not be able to see what I was putting on paper as my eyes would have been clouded by pain or immense anger. Sometimes I would read and then destroy it.

Writing poetry is a way to express my innermost feelings about my struggles and to give gratitude to God who heard my many cries and delivered me from all my adversities.

I am a living testimony that God is able to heal us in every area of our lives—mentally, emotionally, physically, psychologically and spiritually. I believe in my heart that all which I have been through is the key to help unshackle someone else going through turmoil and low self-worth.

On that basis, knowing that a mandate has been given to me to reach the broken, the hopeless and the lost through these words inspired by God, I decided to compile these poems to share my journey. Most importantly, this book is to make the hands of God visible.

When Scars Become Beauty Marks

The emotional scar is an evidence of your experience— what you've been through. Once the scar has been identified, it can be the beginning of healing the soul.

Emotional scars when covered oftentimes reflect anger, aggression, unforgiveness and bitterness. Having a true desire to be healed is an important step towards breaking down emotional walls and barriers. This usually leads to a change of attitude, like the smoothing of the skin in the healing process.

Help is usually needed to heal emotional scars. While counselling or the intervention of others assist in the process, true healing can only come from God. "He heals the brokenhearted and binds up their wounds." (Psalm 147:3, NKJV).

Our distinctive perfections make us beautiful. The scars left behind by our wounds are a part of our beauty. In Japan there is an art of mending or repairing broken pottery with lacquer mixed with powdered gold called *kintsugi*. It is said that the philosophy behind the technique is to recognize the history of the object. Like the broken pottery, we all can be like *kintsugi*, beautifully mended. All we have to do is give ourselves to the Potter's wheel and allow Him to turn us into masterpieces.

God has a plan for you. If you have the desire to overcome your struggles, failures and past, I am here to tell you that you are not alone. As you read through these pages, I pray that the Holy Spirit will do a work of transformation and restoration in you through the renewing of your mind. Use the ***My Beauty Marks*** section to reflect on your own experiences.

I believe that this book will act as a seed planted in you, watered by your desire to grow and sustained by your will to fight to become who God has called you to be. At the end of it all, may God be glorified.

The Scars Within

Listen

Can you hear my cry? Not the sound of my voice
screaming, but my very thoughts towards living,
the thoughts of wanting to hide as I believe
that the bruises and scars of my emotions
are as visible as the promise of the rainbow. The cry
of giving up as I feel as if I'm not good enough.
Can you see the tears of my heart in my fainted smile?
I refuse to make eye contact not because I'm rude
but because I'm fearful that you will see the pain
in my soul that howls like a weeping willow.

Can you hear the questions in my mind, wondering
what my purpose is, will I walk in it
and will it be my time?
A path which has been destined for me, as I am
ordained before time to take such strides.
Can you hear the cries and moans from a mother,
a sister or even just a random caregiver?
Someone who chooses to see the greater good in people
and has decided to counteract hatred with love.
Can you hear the cry of the mental battles from
negative seeds planted and taken as gospel?

The cry to break free from all the invisible
chains around my heart and mind
as they have me in restrain.

Can you hear the cry from the battles I have been
fighting just to fit in? I feel so unaccepted.
I cry because I'm broken, I cry because of
the doubts that plague my mind.
I try to figure a way out.
I cry because my spirit mourns despite the wealth
of the flesh. I'm angry because I'm lost,
I'm hurting because I'm confused, I'm
defeated because of my unbelief.
Oh, by the way,
That's the girl I used to be. The Lord heard
my cries and attended to my needs.

Can you hear the cry of a victor who refused
to be a victim? I bellow the sound of triumph
as I stand in the gap for others.
I echo the cry of triumph, believing that my
Heavenly Father will use me for the exact
purpose for which I was created.
Do you hear the cry of someone who
stands tall even after multiple falls?
The cry of appreciation of grace, my cries have changed.
I now work to see my Heavenly Father's face.
No matter how battered and bruised I get, I have
made up my mind to run and finish this race.

My Beauty Marks

One Last Dance

The sounds are familiar, the moves are enticing
and the friendly faces so inviting.
It is like riding a bike,
one, two, and I am ready to go. I never missed a beat.
I have not forgotten how the music made me high
and the bass and strings brought healing
to my bones.
I plant my feet yet they move without my consent.
The sound of the drum strikes my spinal
nerves and all I can hear, taste and feel
is that rhythm that he plays.
Am I a fool to dance to the devil's beat?

I made a vow as I walked away from my former
life and all the ungodly ways I once knew,
yet I'm here again, right back where I met You.
My mind and emotions are entangled in the past.
How do I move forward, how do I truly let go?
I have no intention of staying here,
but just to whet my appetite
to see if I can calm the anxieties of my
heart and the tingling of my flesh
that gets so excited once exposed to the familiar step.

I remember the high feeling that comes with
just a little sip of the things I used to do
for temporary healing.
As I came crashing down and reality would set in,
my high felt like an altitude that would cause
a struggle to breathe in air so thin.
There is a thin line between life and death,
yet I dance on cord like a tight rope walker in a circus.

Being so tangled in my past it is now my present,
I begin to lose focus.
Farther and farther away I stray
not realizing that I'm going after a bait.
The enemy dangles my favourite flavour of sin
knowing what it takes for him to win.
I played Russian roulette with my life,
ignoring the consequences, the epicentre of my actions
due to the desire to fulfill the lust of the flesh.

I thought I had it all under control so I
could run in and get back out,
however, blindsided by my physical senses—
my sight was made obscure by temporary feelings.
The girl I am now is heading back to who she used to be,
a simple touch of the fire engulfed my body
and though it felt good, my soul is sad
because I have tasted of the Lord
and I miss what I had.

The seed has been planted so I watered it with repentance
and made up in my mind to change my stance.
Like a cat with its tail on fire I run to my Father,
in Him, I'm sheltered from danger.
I now dwell in His presence and my heart says yes,
I'm happy that He once again delivers me from my mess.

My Beauty Marks

Sinful Nature

Born with a sinful nature
it would seem as if I didn't have a chance.
Twice defeated, this is my nature
and the things of the flesh are so enticing.

I have danced on stages that I don't belong,
I have listened to the words and danced to the tunes.
They minister to the flesh and put me in a right groove.

Now the music is fading and all I can hear is my thoughts.
Why do You love me?
How can You love me
when I have fallen short?
I have fallen from Your image that I have been created in.
I have opened doors that are forbidden,
how can You love me when I can't see
my worth? How can You love me
when I don't know the person looking
back at me in the mirror?
How can You love me
when I have made a vow?—
and like a dog to its vomit, I went
right back where I started.

My sinful nature longed for the familiar
and I whet its appetite with just a
conversation or a strong love song.
Now my flesh is happy and my spirit man cries.

My nature is not who I am,
why do I fail to see that in the Garden
of Eden, I was called woman?
The one with the promise, the one that will stand.
All I need to do is take His hand.

A love so great that he did a trade—
I should have paid for my sin but He
sent His son to take my place.
Jesus bled and died,
the just for the unjust.

Grace is extended and I can't comprehend it,
to ask for forgiveness and our lives will be mended.
I can't out-sin God's love, no matter
how far I go or how low I get.
His love is enough.
His love restores my identity and leads me into my destiny,
His love mends my brokenness.
When I was at a place where I felt like a complete mess
He calls me His child and my DNA has changed.
My life has been rewritten and all
my sins have been forgiven.
I can now testify of God's goodness and grace.

I'm now challenged to live so that my life can be a light.
The godly character must shine through.
God, I now realize that my life is not
about me, it's all about You.

My Beauty Marks

A Seed Is a Seed

No season, situation, climate or given location
can alter the characteristics of a seed.
No matter the cruel environment or the misplacement,
a seed is a seed.
One created to flourish and to reproduce,
putting its existence to use.
Beaten down by the cruel elements of life, riding the waves
waiting until the tide is right.
Broken down and covered by dirt is only
a part of the germination process
but that will never change its worth.
Feeling down and struggling to find your
footing, doesn't mean you lack gifting.
A seed thrown on the concrete and trodden upon
will have a different outcome than the same seed
placed in the soil and nurtured to its potential.

A seed is a seed,
but whether you wither and die or grow to bear fruit,
your association and foundation will
determine if you spring forth root.
Like a tree planted by the rivers of
water we are called to be,

to bring forth much fruit for all to see.
The unearthing of our gifting and walking in our calling
is all dependent on who is doing the farming.
A good farmer waters his seed with faith and expectation,
supplying nutrients of edification,
eradicating
diseases of doubt and negativity
and pruning the plants for longevity.

If you are a seed with the desire to grow
to create shelter for the hurting,
with the branches of experiences you have acquired, one
can learn from you, instead of taking individual chances.
Now it all makes sense why you were
buried but could not die,
when you are connected to the true
source you must bring forth life.

My Beauty Marks

Mending in the Making

She Doesn't Love Me

How can you love her when she doesn't love me?
You said I was created to be great but
she says that's a terrible mistake.
You said I can be all things but that
information was not passed on to me.
Instead, she constantly reminds me of my
limitations and for that I approach my goals
with hesitation.

She says I'm not smart enough, I'm not well-rounded,
I feel like a dog that has been impounded.
My goals are farfetched, my dreams unrealistic.
The lies have now become systematic.
She keeps me chained with her negative words.
Eyes wide shut, my dreams pass me by.
I'm pushed to the point where even
You I would want to deny.
Even Your love and grace I feel as if I don't deserve.

She has caused me to hold my head up,
shoulders back but my spirit bowed.
My shoulders are squared but how
much more can I truly bear?

I exist without living and she feels
safe having me in this prison.
The darkness seems long and her torment she prolongs.
She screams so loud even in a crowd, am
I the only one who can hear her?
"You will never be who He has created you to be.
Your very thoughts are a fantasy."

Her words cut like a knife.
She hates me because I remind her of who she was,
she fears me because of who I might become.
The person I see looks just like me
as I stare in the mirror, she looks right back at me.
I can see her pain and her hurt, her mistakes,
her abuse, her doubts, her constant misuse.
I see her fears, her tears, her broken
heart and her weary thoughts.

I reach out to her because as I journey along
both of us need to become one.
In His likeness and image I was made, but she
fights back because she doesn't believe that
someone so broken can become a masterpiece.

It gets better each and every day and now she is
seeing me for who I am supposed to be—
but it's not an easy journey.
You have told me all that I'm not, you have
told me all that I could not be.

Like a dark cloud you were cast over my hope
as I allowed your words to enfold me
like a blanket on a cold night.
I held your words to be true and refused
to step out into the light.
"Where I am is where I belong,"
I would repeat to myself like a happy song.
I felt like I was sinking deep into a place
that was specially designed for me.
No matter what I'm going through, no one
will be able to understand or set me free.

My place of distress now feels like home,
pain and disappointment are all I have ever known.
I have walked a path that's dark and lonely,
praying and hoping that one day this
will be a redemption story.
I was so broken I could not see my worth
and for that I thought that which was given
to me was what I truly deserved.

Now the Son has come and shun His light,
calling me from darkness.
My identity is not in what you think of me.
Who I am is not shaped by your thoughts
or your perception of my destiny.

I am fearfully and wonderfully made;
I am the head and not the tail,
the one that was lost but has now taken her rightful place.

Excuse me while I sit at the table and dine with my Father.
Finding who I am is now a barrier to your lying words.
My identity repels your negativity.
Watch me as I use your stones to create a platform
to set the captive free and reach for girls
who are just like me.

My Beauty Marks

Optical Illusion

I'm confused,
I don't know what I'm feeling or seeing.
The bittersweet of things have me
emotionally tranquilized.
Should I believe your words or your actions?
It's not always bad because at times
you provide satisfaction.
Should I believe your touch, the gifts that you
give or the words that you whisper?
Killing me softly as you enticed,
it is only your ego that matters.
Your touch is as cold as ice and cuts like a knife,
your words are stifling and as intense
as a dagger to my heart.

You have kept me quiet with all your goodies
and brainwashed me to believe that, the fact
that there is no scar you are not a bully.
The emotional and psychological pain have
caused heart palpitations and I'm so scared
I give no reactions.
I have given you power,
you have caused me to believe that I am weak.

I have told myself that I need you when truth be told
I need me.

I need me to realize that this is toxic
and your actions have become a calculated practice.
I need me to realize that my happiness is
not for sale and no amount of gift
should keep me quiet about your abuse.

You try to wrap me around your finger, and as I
look at you all I can see is a complete stranger.
I made the excuses; I believed you would
change but you are aroused
by your pathetic games of a puppet master.
The sweet has now become bitter and I
realize that my life truly matters.
All you might see is someone to manipulate
and I have been losing sight of who I am.
Your tokens are sweet but your touch is poison.
You have gotten into my head and caused
me to lose my sense of reason.
I have sat quietly and made all the excuses,
but now that I have come to the realization,
nothing is stopping me from breaking free.

Your gifts are not worth it, and I know in
my heart that I truly don't deserve it.
You don't know my worth hence the
reason for your actions

and then you walk with a broad chest
as if you are a real man.
You can take back all that you have given me
because nothing is worth my sanity.
I cut myself loose and untie the noose,
I walk away with my experience and
clear distinction of my value.
I have paid a tremendous price but I now
realize that not all that glitters is gold.

My Beauty Marks

Dream

Am I not allowed to dream?
To reach for the stars and dance on the moon?
To paint my dreams and rise above adversities?

Am I not allowed to dream?
To believe that there is more to life than this?
To believe that there is more to me than which is seen?
Purpose knocks on the inside
and yet I ignore it.
Without a doubt opportunity screams
but I choose to shut out the shout.

Am I not allowed to dream?
Believing that one day
there will be compensation for all my pain,
there will be a reward for all trials,
there will be evidence of all the 'I cans'.

Am I not allowed to believe?
To believe that if I can think it,
I can achieve it?
To believe that I am delivered by
the Almighty's strong hand
and one day I will stand before great men?

Am I not allowed to rejoice?
Even through trials and tribulations,
I smile.
Through conflict I remain calm,
through the negative words spoken over my life.

I remain resolute to the purpose that God has placed in me.
I thank Him that He has properly positioned me and
placed people in the right place—entrusting them with me,
my destiny helpers.
Above all that I see and all the things
that have happened to me,
I have learned to have a posture of gratitude and with that,
thankfulness is now my attitude.

My Beauty Marks

The One Is Me

I waited on the promises and the
prophecies I have received.
I looked on with expectancy sometimes on bended knees.
I wonder if my position is out of line
as I pace the floor asking,
"when will it be my time?"
I have gotten the Word over and over again
that my breakthrough is at hand
and all I need to do is believe in His words and stand.

I stand with eyes wide open as an excited child
waiting on the gift that her dad had promised.
Imagine the disappointment when
there seemed to be no gift.
Did the delivery man miss my address?
Or is it just not my time yet?

Each day I anticipate that one person—who
will bring the change to my season?
That one person who will sow a seed
and create a harvest so great
help would be needed to reap.

I pray for that one person who will bring my turn around.
God!!!! Where are You?
Where is my one?
The one who will ease my pain
and cause the sun to chase away the rain.

I am waiting on You as my strength grows dim,
only to realize that all I needed is deep within.
The one to make a difference and create the ripple effect
is me.
I was blinded by the things I was seeing
and all the things I was hearing.
I have caused my sight to block my vision.

The one that I have been anticipating
and desperately trying to identify all along, all I
needed was to take a look in the mirror to see,
that one is me.

My Beauty Marks

Don't Lose Hope

Like a fighter in the boxing ring, you may have
to dodge when the opponent swings.
Bobbing and weaving through the punches
of life, knowing that you can't give up,
you have to put up a fight.
The distractions of superficial satisfaction cheer
on as you rise and fall, covered in bruises
yet you stand tall.

Your knees are weak but you refuse to crumble,
leaning on the promises keep you stable.
The path seems lonely and your fire grows dim,
the courage needed buried deep within.
The time is quiet as they look on with expectation,
wondering if you can go another round, or
will the towel be thrown to the ground?
The scream of your fear has become extremely loud,
yet the face of hope can be seen in the crowd.

Feelings are like shadows they come and
they go, they are not tangible,
they serve to remind that there is light.
Don't lose hope when others may doubt.

A hill can become a plain if you just open your mouth.
The punches keep coming and you feel like falling,
don't go down, and do not lose the
vitality just keep on moving.
Striving for a better tomorrow will help
us to endure the hardship today
this too shall pass one given day.

Never accept defeat,
through hope you have already won,
the soul is continually energized as the spirit cheers on.
Hope builds paths through rugged terrain
and with great pleasure it will have
you dancing in the rain.
Never lose hope,
your tomorrow is beyond the daybreak.
The brokenness you feel
can be mended once you allow the light to shine in.

My Beauty Marks

Lord I know that Your promises are true
and for that when I'm tried and I don't
know what to do, I will wait.
My patience grows thin as fear and doubt try to win
but I will wait.

As time goes by and seasons change,
I know that Your promises will never fail.
The mountains seem higher and the tunnel seems darker,
I will wait on You my Way Maker.

I believe the plans You have for me to be true,
so I hold onto Your unchanging hands.
Truly, there is nothing else to do.

My faith may waver and my hope grows dim.
There is a battle I fight deep within.

I will wait knowing that our timing is different
and it is when You say that takes preeminence.

I will wait not with a backup plan,
I will wait not with an option to lean on.
I will wait with knees bowed and hands clasped,
I will wait knowing that one day
You will come through at last.
I will wait knowing that patience is a virtue
and virtue is grace
and waiting on You is seeking your face.

My Beauty Marks

Rest

The delicate fabric caresses the hard-textured surface
as her body welcomes the unfavourable foundation.
One that produces discomfort and yet stability.
She rests upon the hardcore roughness given to her,
yet without a flinch she holds her composure.
She angles her body as she uses it to answer the questions.
The anatomical structure of her face says she is at peace.

The colour of her dress so white that it glistens,
highlights the blood red blocks that
have now become her bed.
Though they were hurled at her she
used them as a bed linen
stuffed with the wool shaven from a sheep.

Unbothered, she is as she was promised sweet rest.
She refused to fight and though you consider it messy,
she hands it over and there she takes her rest.

My Beauty Marks

Prison Break

Clothed in righteousness that's my raiment,
who the Son sets free is free indeed.
Then why do I hear the chains of my past trailing me
as they glide over the humps and bumps of my mistakes?
They would want to tangle my mind,
making such a loud jingle.
My past rings a bell calling the pupil back to
class, it takes every fight to stand steadfast.

My mouth says I am free, I confidently
repeat that which was said to me;
my mind says otherwise.
I'm held by my minute thinking,
captive by the thoughts of others knowing
where I am coming from,
captive by the fact that my parents were limited.
The chains of my thoughts have entangled
my progress, like a serpent wrapping my
mind restricting mental movement.

I hear the voice inside my head calling to be set free
as the darkness and the air around me reek a toxic gas,

odour of hopelessness, a fragrance of disbelief,
the pungent smell causes dreams to wither
like leaves of a tree that lack nutrients.
My mental prison had me paralyzed, only because
I spoke the words but did not allow them
to resonate in my soul, to take root and
shoot branches so firm for all to see,
so that, others may glorify the God who I say is in me.

Now I dwell in His presence and the
walls of my prison are shaken.
I now believe that I shall have what I say,
I'm fearfully and wonderfully made.
I shall dream again and accomplish
what I was placed on earth to do.
I am set free my mind is renewed; I
now declare a prison break.

My Beauty Marks

Good Morning

The night has been long as the storm seems to tarry.
The winds of trials and tribulations whistle
and echo like an angry roaring lion.
The darkness of the clouds blots all rays
of hope like a blanket of smoke
suppressing the effort of progress,
a darkness with the texture of mud
that absorbs any physical light
emitted from a man-made effort of survival.
A darkness that would cause the best
effort and the strongest might
to appear as a strike of a match in an all-island blackout.

The darkness howls,
the sound of defeat as hopelessness rises
like waves triggered by the movements
of the earth's tectonic plates,
causing the stirring of the ocean's floor.
The waves of despair shake the foundation of my very core,
washing ashore doubt and fear
leaving behind the silt of frustration.
I compensate my mental lack and inabilities by
satisfying the flesh and dressing the pain

with an optical illusion,
hoping to soothe the heart and relieve the
strain of my perception and interpretation
of what life is supposed to be.

With loss of sight in the darkness and a blurred vision,
I have become a prey of my own limitations.
I retreated for cover, battering up the doors
of my dreams with low self-esteem
and thoughts of impossibilities.
I guarded the windows of my destiny with
debris collected over the years
as I have travelled a path of inadequacies.
My carnal mind oppressed my spirit man as the
flesh engaged in battles it can never win.

I am now left with no choice
but to press beyond feelings and what I'm seeing,
knowing that there is a greater Being.
I connect with my creator, the One who
extends mercies and favour.
The wind and the waves obey Him as
He rolls the dark clouds away,
bringing forth a new day.
A day filled with hope and possibilities,
one that causes the spirit of God to
override all improbabilities.

My Beauty Marks

As the Author in the beginning, You
are the Author 'til the end.
The horizon echoes Your praises and
shows Your handy work.
Like an artist, You used Your brush
and painted hope in the sky.
The cloud dresses the heavens
like a highly decorated valance at an exhibition window.
As the sun breaks through the clouds, so
do Your unchanging words ring,
Your promises giving hope to the doubtful.
The ray of the sunlight breaks the darkness
like the light at the end of the tunnel.
A new day has come, the season has
changed, and new life has risen.
The darkness is not real, it is only the absence of light.

I see the work of Your majestic hands
when the fresh air caresses my face.
The birds sing while the trees dance to their own tune,
the morning sun responds with solitude.
The grass in the field stands tall and reaches
for the sun swaying in the breeze

whistling praises unto Your kingdom.
A day that was not promised, I embrace it
and graciously accept this gift of life.
You hold the sun in its place and use
the stars to mark our blessings.
I know that my future is secured in You.
The breaking of dawn is a new day of grace,
a new day of hope, another chance to dream,
to achieve, to love and even after past hurt
love once more.
A new day is a reminder of Your saving grace.
You give Your love to the unlovable and grant
Your peace unto the restless soul—
a reminder of Your love that corrects
my wrong and fuels my soul.

My Beauty Marks

What Mask?

How did I get here?
I feel like I'm living for your expectations as you
feel I need to make some transformation.
You believe that the life I live is not
the one God has intended
because I did not walk the path that you paved.
My talk, my walk does not reflect you, as if you
are the epitome of the Lord's vision for man.
You say that I'm to remove my mask
so that you can see who I am,
taking me on as if I was given to you as a task.

With my mask being removed can you handle my truth,
given that it's not highly decorated and
it's not what you have anticipated?
Can you handle my experiences if I were to
share them with you unadulterated?
That which you call my mask is not to hide who I am,
but to protect self-righteous gods like you by
dancing on your man-made platform.
Not painting the wall for all to see where it is I
used to be doesn't mean I am hiding something. My
past is my past and not a shadow of who I am.

If you ask me to remove my mask, ensure
that your intentions are pure,
your words true and your heart at the right place.
I'm not ashamed of where I used to be as I'm now able to
reach girls who are going through where I used to be.
So that which you call my mask, it's only my experiences.
If they make you uncomfortable or just curious,
my mask is my mask now what is truly your task?
Doing the same thing over and over,
yet expecting different results,
then I wonder why does it seem I am stuck in a rut?

I open myself up to the same things and the
same people who have caused me pain,
believing and hoping that the experience before
would have been different if I gave much more.
Yet you ride on my emotions and pull me apart,
at times it feels as if my chest is ripped
wide open and my heart is exposed.
You take pieces of me and leave holes
like a fence violently attacked,
with nails driven by an angry workman,
and then spontaneously removed as if
they were not part of his plan.
I have made myself available and exposed like a
sailor shipwrecked and abandoned at sea, crying
for help but the only one who hears is me.

My Beauty Marks

Judge Not

You want to be the judge, the jury and the
prosecutor, go ahead and try me.

You place me on a stand as you dissect
and tear apart my intentions,
trying to disprove my reputation.

Before the trial I'm deemed a criminal, guilty
you say as if the law is in your hand.

I'm here because my actions are
different and unpredictable.
The smile on my face is question, while
my facial expressions are obscure.

You want to convict me for your own good,
as I might show you up.
If the eyes are on me then no one sees you.
So you make your move as one who sits in authority.

You tried my character, even my motives.
You question my loyalty without any real objectives.

You place me on the stand because I
look like someone you knew,
or is it because I don't look like you?
They are all the same, a statement you hold to be true.

I thought you were innocent until proven guilty, yet you
interrogate with such animosity and pull me apart
with your tongue coated with hypocrisy.

You highlighted where I have been and who I knew.
Your motives have now caused the light to be on you.

In your questioning and cross references, in
your intentions to expose me for all you see,
you didn't realize, it was a girl you knew—
that wasn't me.

Your honour, I would like to interject—

As I sit here on trial it is clear that the
prosecutor is most upset.
You want someone to pay for the
wrong that was done to you,
even the hurt and the pain that has caused
you to become so bitter too.

Your self-esteem and confidence have fallen above all,
but I can introduce you to someone
who will help you to recover all.

What if the tables turned and you
were placed on the stand?
Would your actions be justified
because you are only a man?

In judging someone,
you leave yourself wide open for all to
see that you are truly broken.

With all that has been said I now rest my case;
my Lord is the One who vindicates.

My Beauty Marks

That Girl

You call me by the girl you used to know,
refusing to accept that she is no longer there.

You keep reminding me of my shortcomings
and where I have been.
A mental battle you try to win.
You try to keep me broken to hinder my growth,
to lower my self-esteem and act as if
you are the only one
who truly knows my worth.

Like a flower in a box
you want to keep me covered.
You said it's for my own good and you wish I understood.
You said the sun would burn my petals
and the rain rot my roots,
yet I yearn to dance in the rain and
have the wind blow my leaves.

I want to put a smile on someone's face and hope in their heart; but how can I when I feel as if I'm falling apart?

This is not who I am anymore,
not the saddened helpless girl that you adore.

I'm a woman with clear identity, big
dreams and great responsibility.
I'm a woman though once broken
I'm now mended.
You were there for my 'been through'
and now you are scared of my break-through.

I am a woman who will hold the hand of a
sister and lighten the path of a brother.
A woman who has now found her calling
and I can now see that you are scared
because I'm no longer backing down.

Before the creation of the earth
plans and provision were made for me,
being great is a part of my destiny.
Watch me rise despite my fall
and watch God get the glory
as I stand tall.

The chains are broken and now I am
free, the chain of mental captivity
and mediocrity.
I am royalty.
You have walked with me
but don't know who I am.
Purpose runs through my vein.
On Christ the solid Rock I stand.

My Beauty Marks

Let my words caress your ears and tug
on your heart as a reminder that
you were never an afterthought.
Yes, these words are for someone who has
been broken and wandered afar off.
A prisoner of her doings, a slave to her sins,
her conscience rebels as her spirit
screams from deep within.
Like the thief on the cross she has
been nailed by her actions,
a just price from a judicial decision.
Lost she was; was this her fate or was it her destiny?

She moved swiftly through the rhythm of
life, beaten down with refusal to bow.
She refuses to bow to that which others see or think of her,
she refuses to bow to her generational legacy.
She sees in herself strength and beauty.
A lost sheep she was and He saw her as His duty
to redeem and restore, giving her insight and
revelation of who she is called to be.

Assurance is what she needs and
that is what He surely gives,
He is bound by His every Word and
cannot go back on His promises.
He paid with His life a transaction that was priceless.
His life for hers, He did that so she might live.
He bore the shame and ridicule so that she
could stand tall and lift her head high.
"I love you," He whispers. "Don't you worry,
my arms are open wide, come in a hurry."
"I will give you hope, joy and strength for the
journey in the days ahead. I believe in you, only
if you would accept that which is true."

He has made all things new.
He died on the cross to bridge the
gap between God and man.
His death made a way,
even the guilty and convicted still have
hope and a chance of a new life.
All we have to do is trade, give Him our
way of life and take His hand.

My Beauty Marks

I am Beauty

Beauty is who I am.
Beauty is who I consciously want to be.
Whenever I look at my reflection, my
Father's handy work I see.

He blew in me the breath of life and just
like you I have all the rights,
to experience love and grace given by the One
who reigns over the earth and above.

Beauty is in the hope of my smile.
In my shoes I dare you to walk a mile.
The struggles are hard, the toil seems rough.
But there is a time when my Dad says, "enough!"

Beauty is who I am,
in the reach of my arm, to the one who is less fortunate
and now their hearts are far from being warm.

Beauty is the life that I live, even the
very things that I give—
A word of encouragement or a meal for nourishment,
a hug, a pat on the shoulder
or just by saying 'chin up, God's chosen soldier'.

Beauty is who I am,
in my thoughts not just of me
but of you whether we are friends or far apart.

Beauty describes God's masterpiece,
someone who others may see as the least.
Chosen to be a beauty, not by the clothes that you wear
or the colour of your hair.
But let Christ be seen in you.
Show someone you care.

My Beauty Marks

I promise to love you like no one else could. A
love that springs forth joy and assertiveness,
a love like raindrops pouring on a soil that
has been abused by the brutal sun.
I promise to love you as a payback to your darkest
times, through your loneliness, disappointments and
when you seem to have failed life's daily tests.

I will love you back to life,
I will love you from your weakest point
until you have found your strength.
I will pour into you words of affirmation, I
will revive you like blood transfusion.
Loving you is changing your vision,
working daily to a greater plan.

I will love you so that even in your
dark clouds you get excited,
with your focus on what is to come and not what is.
A love so pure it knows no bounds, loving
you until you turn your life around.
I am going to love you so that when I look
in the mirror you smile back at me.

I have tasted the bitterness of the tears and
felt the rhythmic beating of the heart
racing to get away from the pain that causes the
chest to tighten and the lungs to collapse.

I'm going to love you despite the person I see,
because where you are now is not where you intend to be.
Your present location is not your final
destination, to make a move
it first takes mind elevation.
Taking into consideration that for a
mental transformation to occur,
emancipation from the psychological bondage and baggage
of all the past hurt needs to be placed in the disposal.
I'm going to love you like you have never been
hurt, in loving you, it will restore your worth.

My Beauty Marks

Broken to Beauty Marks

I have gotten a few battle scars and by the
grace of God I have come this far.
My tears were once my dearest friends
and no matter how good it was,
I knew we would somehow meet again.
I lived a life expecting the worst.
I believed that nothing good ever happens to me
and my smile would always turn into a frown.
I dwell on the pain to avoid the joy,
believing that joy would be short-
lived based on experiences.
I have been broken to the point where
I believe that this is it,
there could never be a possible comeback.

My body started following the leading of my mind
and gave into the mode of slumber and non-productivity.
My body agreed that where I am, I would never elevate.
After all, I have all the right reasons to be hopeless,
I know the people who should be blamed.
I like throwing my pity party as it only
made sense why I seem to be stuck.

I have the reason for lack of growth, I have
the right answers to why I never smiled.
I bask in my bitterness as I identify
the reason for my brokenness.
I have been so low, there is no further to go.

I waited to find someone who cared, and as
help came it was rejected because of fear.
Then the Lord whispered softly to me,
"I will never give you more than you can bear,
take My hand I truly care".
I took His hand as He led me along,
the journey and the path that I have taken became clear
that it was a part of all that God had for me in the making.
The process was only to help the progress for the promise.
Now I embrace my brokenness as beauty marks;
they are a reminder of where I have been and called
forth who I'm supposed to be from within.

My Beauty Marks

Crossword Puzzle

Down:
1. Being set free from a situation.
3. I know who I am.
4. An expectation of a particular thing to happen.
6. The process of returning to your former condition.
9. Jehovah Tsidkenu.
11. The greatest of the three that remains.
14. To develop over a period of time.
15. Having the ability to function effectively.
18. The capacity to withstand great pressure.

Across:
2. Grace.
5. The value ascribed to oneself.
7. Revelation 12:11.
8. 2 Corinthians 1:20.
10. To consciously or intentionally do something.
12. Being worthy of honour and respect.
13. regain through the exchange of payment.
16. The lack makes it impossible to please God.
17. The reason for which i was created.
19. What is to be must be.
20. Compelled by the need to accomplish a goal.

Crossword Puzzle

Down:
1. Being set free from a situation.
3. I know who I am.
4. An expectation of a particular thing to happen.
6. The process of returning to your former condition.
9. Jehovah Tsidkenu.
11. The greatest of the three that remains.
14. To develop over a period of time.
15. Having the ability to function effectively.
18. The capacity to withstand great pressure.

Across:
2. Grace.
5. The value ascribed to oneself.
7. Revelation 12:11.
8. 2 Corinthians 1:20.
10. To consciously or intentionally do something.
12. Being worthy of honour and respect.
13. regain through the exchange of payment.
16. The lack makes it impossible to please God.
17. The reason for which i was created.
19. What is to be must be.
20. Compelled by the need to accomplish a goal.

About The Author

Racquel Ricketts-Lee is a trained educator with over eleven years teaching experience in Cosmetology. She has been working in the beauty industry for over seventeen years. Racquel serves as the youth pastor at Kingdom Builders Open Bible Church in Jamaica, and studies Biblical and Pastoral Studies at the College of Theological and Interdisciplinary Studies (CTIS). Racquel has a passion for broken women but more so young girls. Her work within the beauty industry has afforded her the opportunity to minister and pour into these young lives. Whether working on set for a television series, a photo-shoot or a runway show, her ministry expands beyond the four walls of the Church.

www.ingramcontent.com/pod-product-compliance
Lightning Source LLC
Chambersburg PA
CBHW060818050426
42449CB00008B/1714